Contents

Key

Key

* easy

** medium

*** difficult

Greek food

The largest part of Greece is called the mainland, but the country also includes over 2000 islands, scattered throughout the Aegean and Ionian seas. Only 151 of these islands have people living on them, though.

In the past

Several civilizations have lived in Greece at different times over the past 2000 years. These include the Ancient Greeks, the Ancient Romans and the Phoenicians – traders who sailed to the Far East and brought back spices. Each civilization has cooked and prepared food slightly differently.

Around the country

Summer in Greece is extremely hot, but the winters can be cold and rainy. The main crops have always been wheat, olives and grapes. Much of the land is mountainous, making farming difficult. Sheep and goats wander over the slopes, but only tough plants, such as thyme and rosemary, grow well there.

In more sheltered areas, farmers grow fruit and vegetables, such as lemons and aubergines. They also grow almonds, pistachios, walnuts and pine nuts. Many people keep bees, using their honey to sweeten recipes.

▲ *With over 15,000km of coastline, fishing is an important Greek industry.*

As meat can be scarce, it is usually served with rice, lentils and bread to make a small piece feed more people. Cooks use sheep and goat's milk to make milk, creamy yoghurt and cheese. Many people in Greece belong to the Greek Orthodox Church, which forbids people from eating meat on several days of the year. Greek people often cook meat for special festivals, such as Easter. Then, a family might roast a whole lamb.

Greek meals

In Greece, meals are often a selection of cooked vegetables and yoghurt dishes, called a mezze (pronounced *metsay*). These might be followed by fish or meat which is **marinated** in olive oil with herbs and vegetables, and then **grilled** or **baked**. Cooks often barbecue fish and meat with lemons, tomatoes or spices. Desserts include fruit, such as figs, melons, dates and oranges, or yoghurt and honey.

Ingredients

melons

raisins

aubergine

courgettes

peppers

cos lettuce

parsley

feta cheese

olives

lemons

grapes

almonds

figs

garlic

tomatoes

rosemary

mint

dates

cinnamon sticks

pine nuts

Aubergines

Greek cooks stuff aubergines with a filling based on rice. They also **bake** them slowly, then **blend** them with olive oil, onions and garlic to make a creamy salad dip. You can buy aubergines at most supermarkets and greengrocers.

Almonds

Almonds were first brought to Greece centuries ago, by traders from Asia. They are used in many sweet and **savoury** Greek recipes. Peeling off their brown skin is tricky, so buy blanched (ready skinned), ones if you can. They are available from supermarkets.

Feta

Feta is a cheese made from sheep or goat's milk. Outside Greece, it is kept fresh in brine (salty water).

If feta tastes too salty to you, soak it in cold water overnight before using it. You can buy it in larger supermarkets and delicatessens.

Cumin and coriander

These two spices are often used together in savoury Greek dishes. Neither is a hot spice. The seeds are usually lightly **fried** or **toasted** before they are added to dishes.

Herbs

Basil, dill, mint, oregano, parsley, rosemary, thyme and bay leaves are all used to flavour Greek dishes. These herbs are available dried in supermarkets, and fresh in larger ones.

Olives

Olives are yellow to start with, then they become green. Farmers pick them at this point, and then leave them to ripen more in the sun until they turn purple, brown and eventually black. Most Greek dishes use black olives. You can buy whole olives with the stone in them, or pitted olives, with the stone taken out. They are available in jars or cans, or loose, from the **delicatessen** counter of most supermarkets.

Vine leaves

These are large leaves from grape vines. They are usually packed in brine (salty water) in plastic pouches. Look for them at larger supermarkets.

Yoghurt

Greek yoghurt is very thick and creamy. It is usually made from **pasteurized** sheep or goat's milk. It is very thick, because it has cream added to it. It is available in tubs from most supermarkets.

Before you start

Kitchen rules

There are a few basic rules you should always follow when you are cooking:

- Ask an adult if you can use the kitchen.
- Some cooking processes, especially those involving hot water or oil, can be dangerous. When you see this sign, take extra care or ask an adult to help.
- Wash your hands before you start.
- Wear an apron to protect your clothes, and tie back long hair.
- Be very careful when using sharp knives.
- Never leave pan handles sticking out in case you knock them.
- Always wear oven gloves to lift things in and out of the oven.
- Wash fruit and vegetables before using them.

How long will it take?

Some of the recipes in this book are quick and easy, and some are more difficult and take longer. The strip across the top of the right hand page of each recipe tells you how long it will take you to cook each dish from start to finish. It also shows how difficult each dish is to make: every recipe is either * (easy), ** (medium) or *** (difficult).

Quantities and measurements

You can see how many people each recipe will serve at the top of each right hand page. You can multiply or divide the quantities if you want to cook for more or fewer people.

Ingredients for recipes can be measured in two different ways. Metric measurements use grams and millilitres. Imperial measurements use ounces and fluid ounces. This book uses metric measurements. If you want to convert these into imperial measurements, see the chart on page 44.

In the recipes you will see the following abbreviations:

tbsp = tablespoon   g = grams
tsp = teaspoon   ml = millilitres

Utensils

To cook the recipes in this book, you will need these utensils (as well as essentials, such as spoons, plates and bowls):

- baking tray
- electric whisk
- food processor or blender
- large frying pan (heavy-based, if possible)
- lemon squeezer
- measuring jug
- chopping board
- small screw-topped jar
- saucepans with lids
- set of scales
- sharp knife
- measuring spoons
- 1.5 litre and 2 litre shallow ovenproof dishes
- 20cm square baking tin
- 20cm round cake tin
- 4 skewers (metal)

 Whenever you use kitchen knives, be very careful.

Aubergine and lentil soup

In Greece, many people grow aubergines in their gardens. Aubergines can have purple skins, creamy skins or purple skins flecked with white. They must always be cooked before you eat them. Look out for firm, shiny skin. An aubergine with wrinkly skin may taste bitter.

What you need

1 small aubergine
40g brown lentils
1 onion
1 clove garlic
1 tbsp oil
1 vegetable stock cube
3 tbsp tahini paste (made from sesame seeds)
salt and pepper

What you do

1 **Preheat** the oven to 180°C/350°F/gas mark 4. Put the aubergine on a baking tray and **bake** it for 30 minutes. Leave it to **cool**.

2 Meanwhile, put the lentils and 600ml cold water into a pan. Bring to the **boil**. Boil the lentils for 10 minutes and then **simmer** them for 10 minutes. (Top up with extra hot water if the lentils look as if they are drying up. Don't add salt – it makes lentils tough!)

3 **Peel** and **chop** the onion and garlic.

4 Heat the oil in a frying pan, add the onion and **fry** it over a gentle heat for 3 minutes.

5 Add the garlic and cook for a further 2 minutes.

6 Cut the aubergine in half. Scoop out the creamy flesh.

(!) 7 **Drain** the lentils and spoon them into a blender or food processor. Add the aubergine flesh, tahini, onion and garlic. Crumble in the stock cube.

8 **Blend** the mixture until it is smooth. Carefully stir in 300ml hot water.

9 Pour the soup into a saucepan and simmer it for 2 minutes.

10 Add a little salt and pepper. Serve with warm crusty bread or pitta bread (see page 12).

Pitta breads

In Greece, flat pitta breads are used to scoop up food, or they are filled with salads and cooked meat.

What you need

350g strong flour
½ tsp salt
7g sachet easy blend
  dried yeast
2 tbsp olive oil

What you do

1 Put the flour, salt, oil and yeast into a food processor. Put the lid on and process, pouring 200ml warm water slowly through the funnel until a soft dough forms.

2 Process for a further 3 minutes. Put the dough into a bowl. Rub a little olive oil over a sheet of clingfilm and cover the bowl with it. Leave the dough in a warm place for about 40 minutes to rise.

3 Cut the dough into 8 equal-sized pieces.

4 Roll one piece out with a rolling pin until it makes a circle about 20cm wide. Fold it in half and shape it into a teardrop shape, about 20 by 10cm. Lift it onto a baking tray.

5 Repeat this for all 8 pieces of dough. Cover them with the oiled clingfilm and leave them in a warm place for 30 minutes.

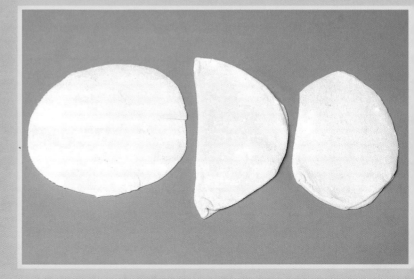

6 **Preheat** the oven to 220°C/450°F/gas mark 8. Take the clingfilm off and **bake** the pitta for about 7 minutes.

7 Sprinkle some water onto a clean tea towel and spread it over the pitta breads. This will keep some steam inside them as they **cool**.

8 To warm the pitta breads up, put them into a toaster or under a **grill**. Hold them with a clean tea towel to protect your hands from hot steam when you split them.

▲ *You can either fill pitta breads with hot food, or **slice** them into pieces and serve them with salad.*

Tzaziki with grilled vegetables

Tzaziki (pronounced *satseekee*) is a mixture of chopped cucumber and yoghurt. It sometimes has chopped mint and garlic added to it. In Greece, it is served with pitta bread or with a selection of other dishes.

Because Greek cooks usually cook only once a day, they might serve the grilled vegetables hot, or **chill** them and serve them cold.

What you need

For the roasted vegetables:
1 red pepper
1 yellow pepper
1 courgette
½ an aubergine
2 tbsp olive oil

For the tzaziki:
½ a cucumber
150ml Greek yoghurt
1 clove garlic (optional)
salt and pepper

What you do

1 Cut the peppers into quarters. Cut out and throw away the stalk and the seeds.

2 Lay the pepper pieces skin side up onto a **grill** pan.

3 Cut the courgette and aubergine into 1cm thick **slices**. Put them onto the grill pan.

4 Brush the vegetables with some of the olive oil.

5 Cook the vegetables under a medium grill until they brown. Using a fork, turn the courgette and aubergine over. Brush with a little more oil and continue to cook for a few minutes.

6 When the peppers' skins have turned black, put them into a small plastic box and put the lid on. Leave them to **cool**.

7 **Peel** off the peppers' skins.

8 Wash the cucumber and cut it into ½cm thick slices. Cut the slices into ½cm thick strips. Cut these into ½cm cubes.

9 Put the cucumber cubes into a sieve and put it over a bowl for 5 minutes to **drain**.

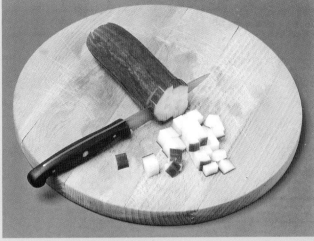

10 Stir the cucumber into the yoghurt. Peel and crush the garlic and stir into the tzaziki (if using garlic).

11 Add a little salt and pepper, and spoon into a bowl. Serve with the grilled vegetables.

15

Feta cheese salad

During the hot Greek summer, many people eat in outdoor restaurants called tavernas. Feta cheese salad, often called a 'Greek salad', is a popular dish in every taverna. It is either served on its own, with bread, or with a main course.

What you need

For the salad:
½ a cos lettuce, or
   1 little gem lettuce
½ a cucumber
4 tomatoes
1 onion
150g feta cheese
50g pitted black olives

*For the **dressing**:*
4 tbsp olive oil
2 tbsp lemon juice

What you do

1 Cut the lettuce in half lengthways. Wash the leaves and gently pat them dry with a clean tea towel. Cut them into 1cm thick **slices**.

2 Wash the cucumber and cut it into 1cm thick slices. Cut each slice into quarters.

3 Wash the tomatoes and **chop** them into small pieces. **Peel** and slice the onion.

4 Cut the feta cheese into 1cm cubes.

5 Put the chopped lettuce, cucumber and tomatoes into a bowl. Add the feta cheese and olives.

6 Put the oil and lemon juice into a small screw-topped jar. Just before serving the salad, shake well and pour the dressing over the salad.

EATING OUTSIDE

Every town and village in Greece has at least one taverna. In the summer, diners enjoy their meals surrounded by trailing vines and pots of brightly coloured flowers. Often, musicians play traditional Greek music while people eat.

Moussaka

Moussaka is one of the most famous Greek dishes. For a **vegetarian** version, start at step 3, replacing the lamb mince with 500g chopped mushrooms and an extra courgette.

What you need

500g minced lamb
1 large onion
1 tbsp olive oil
2 cloves garlic
1½ tsp ground cumin
1½ tsp ground coriander
1 tsp dried thyme
1 courgette
400g can chopped
    plum tomatoes
1 aubergine

For the white sauce:
300ml milk
3 tbsp cornflour

What you do

1 Put the minced lamb into a saucepan and pour in enough cold water to cover it. Bring it to the **boil, cover** it and cook over a medium heat for 5 minutes, stirring occasionally.

(!) **2** Put a sieve over a bowl and carefully pour the mince into it.

(!) **3** **Peel** and **slice** the onions. Heat the oil in a pan and **fry** them over a low heat for 5 minutes.

4 Peel and crush the garlic. Add it to the pan with the drained lamb, cumin, coriander and thyme. Cook for 3 minutes, stirring occasionally.

5 Cut the ends off the courgette. Cut the courgette into 1cm cubes. Add it to the mince with the tomatoes. Cover and **simmer** for 20 minutes.

6 **Preheat** the oven to 190°C/375°F/gas mark 5.

7 Peel the potatoes and cut them into ½cm slices. Put them in a pan, carefully cover them with boiling water and cook them for 5 minutes. **Drain** them.

8 Cut both ends off the aubergine. Cut the aubergine into 1cm thick slices. Fry them in a non-stick frying pan, without any oil, over a low heat for 3 minutes. Using a fish slice, turn them over and cook the other side for 3 minutes.

9 In a small pan, stir a little of the milk into the cornflour to make a smooth paste. Add the rest of the milk. Heat, stirring all the time, until the sauce thickens.

10 Spoon the mince mixture into a 1.5 litre ovenproof dish. Put a layer of aubergine and potato slices on the top. Pour the sauce over the top.

11 **Bake** for 30 minutes. Serve with a salad, if you like.

Burekakia

Burekakia (pronounced *boorekarkeea*) are filo pastry triangles filled with feta cheese and spinach. In Greece, people buy them hot from stalls in the street.

What you need

200g frozen spinach,
  thawed and **drained**
50g feta cheese
½ tsp ground
  cinnamon
2 tbsp fresh
  chopped mint
a little freshly ground
  black pepper
270g packet filo pastry,
  thawed if frozen
50g butter

What you need

1 Put the spinach into a sieve and press out any liquid with a spoon. Tip it onto a chopping board and **chop** it finely. Put it into a bowl.

2 Crumble the feta into the bowl and add the cinnamon, mint and black pepper. Stir well.

3 Lay the filo pastry flat on a chopping board. Cut it into three 9cm by 50cm strips. Cover them with a clean tea towel.

4 Put the butter into a small saucepan. Heat it gently until it melts.

5 Line a baking tray with non-stick baking paper.

6 On a chopping board, brush one strip of filo pastry with melted butter. Put one heaped teaspoonful of the spinach and feta cheese mixture about 2cm from the top, in the middle.

7 Fold the right-hand top corner over the filling and across to the left-hand edge to form a triangle.

8 Fold the triangle down over the pastry immediately below it to form a straight edge along the top again. Fold the pastry triangle down the length of the strip of pastry. Brush the pastry with butter and put onto the baking tray.

9 Repeat steps 6 to 8 to use all the pastry.

10 **Preheat** the oven to 200°C/400°F/gas mark 6. Bake the burekakia for 10 to 12 minutes, or until golden brown. Serve hot or cold.

Popolettes

Greek cooks often use left over boiled potatoes to make these little potato patties filled with onion, cheese and dill.

What you need

250g potatoes
50g feta cheese
2 spring onions
2 tbsp fresh
   chopped dill
½ tsp fennel seeds
2 tbsp olive oil

What you do

1 Peel the potatoes and **chop** them into 3cm cubes. Put them into a pan and cover them with water.

(!) **2** Add a pinch of salt and bring the water to the **boil**. Cook the potatoes for 15 minutes. **Drain** and **mash** them.

3 Crumble the feta cheese into a bowl. Cut the roots and green tops off the spring onions. Chop the onions finely and add them to the feta cheese.

4 Stir in the dill, fennel seeds and mashed potato.

5 On a chopping board, shape the mixture into six patties.

(!) **6** Heat the oil in a frying pan. **Fry** the patties over a medium heat for 3 minutes. Using a fish slice, turn them over to cook the other side.

7 Serve the popolettes hot or cold with **grilled** meat, fish or vegetables.

CRACKED POTATOES

Here is another way Greek cooks serve potatoes. They cook new potatoes until they are tender. Then they drain them, and add two chopped tomatoes, 1 tbsp olive oil, a few mustard seeds and some chopped parsley to the pan. After putting the pan lid on, they shake the potatoes until they crack and the tomato juices soak into them.

Stuffed peppers and tomatoes

In Greece, many people grow peppers and tomatoes in their garden. They ripen quickly in the hot sun. There are many variations on this dish in different areas.

What you need

75g long grain rice
1 red pepper
1 yellow pepper
4 large tomatoes
1 onion
2 cloves garlic
1 tbsp olive oil
½ tsp ground cumin
½ tsp dried thyme
50g currants

What you do

1 Put the rice into a saucepan with 300ml hot water. **Cover** the pan and bring to the **boil**. **Simmer** for 15 minutes, until the rice has soaked up the water.

2 **Preheat** the oven to 190°C/375°F/gas mark 5. Cut the peppers in half through the stalk. Using a teaspoon, scoop out the seeds.

3 Cut the tomatoes into halves. Scoop out the insides, put them into a bowl and **chop** them up.

4 Put the pepper and tomato halves onto a baking tray.

5 **Peel** the onion and the garlic, and **chop** finely.

(!) 6 Heat the oil in a saucepan and **fry** the onion for 3 minutes. Add the garlic, cumin and thyme, and cook for 1 minute.

7 Stir in the chopped tomato and currants. Cook for 2 minutes, then stir in the cooked rice. Spoon the hot mixture into the pepper and tomato halves.

8 **Bake** for 20 minutes. Carefully lift the peppers and tomatoes off the baking tray onto plates with a fish slice.

9 Serve as a **vegetarian** dish, or with cooked meat or fish.

Lamb kebabs

Thousands of sheep graze on the mountainous slopes of Greece, so lamb is easily available. If you prefer, replace the lamb with boneless, skinless chicken breast. Try cooking your kebabs on a barbecue, as many Greek cooks would!

What you need

800g lean, diced lamb
1 onion
1 tbsp fresh oregano
 or 1 tsp dried oregano
few sprigs of rosemary
1 lemon
100ml olive oil
a little salt and pepper

*To **garnish** (optional):*
lemon wedges and
 sprigs of rosemary

What you do

1 Cut off as much white fat as you can from the lamb. Cut the lamb into 3cm cubes and put them into a bowl.

2 **Peel** and **chop** the onion. Add the onion, oregano and rosemary to the lamb.

3 Cut the lemon in half. Using a lemon squeezer, squeeze out the juice. Chop the lemon skin into small pieces.

4 Add the olive oil, the lemon skin and juice, and a little salt and pepper to the lamb. Stir well, **cover** and **chill** for at least 4 hours – overnight, if possible. During this time, the meat soaks up the flavours of the mixture, which is called a **marinade**.

5 Take the lamb out of the marinade. Thread the cubes onto four metal skewers.

6 **Grill** for 8 to 10 minutes, using oven gloves to turn the skewers so that the meat browns evenly. Cut one piece of meat in half to check that it is cooked. You may like it slightly pink or pale brown-coloured in the middle.

7 Serve garnished with rosemary and lemon wedges, if you like, and with a salad and pitta bread.

27

Fish with red pepper and tomato sauce

Fish is very popular in Greece, served with a variety of sauces. In coastal villages, fresh fish is sold on beds of ice outside tavernas, and freshly caught octopus is hung out to dry. If you use frozen fish for this recipe, **thaw** it in the fridge overnight.

What you need

1 red pepper
1 onion
2 cloves garlic
3 tbsp olive oil
400g can plum
   tomatoes
450g firm white fish
   (such as cod or hake)

To garnish:
fresh parsley

What you do

1 Cut the pepper in half and cut out the stalk and the seeds. **Cut** the pepper into quarters.

2 **Grill** the pepper skin side up until the skin starts to blacken. Put it into a plastic box with a lid. Put the lid on, leave the pepper to **cool**, then **peel** the skin off.

3 **Preheat** the oven to 200°F/400°C/gas mark 6. Peel and chop the onion and garlic.

(!) 4 Heat the oil in a saucepan and cook the onion over a gentle heat for 5 minutes. Add the garlic and cook for 2 minutes.

5 Stir in the tomatoes and the peppers, and cook for 5 minutes. Cool slightly, then spoon into a blender or food processor. Put the lid on and process until smooth.

6 Cut the fish into two portions. Wipe a little oil with kitchen paper around an ovenproof dish. Lay the fish in it, pour over the sauce and cover the dish.

7 Cook in the oven for 15 minutes or until the fish is very white and firm. Garnish with parsley and serve with a salad.

Stuffed vine leaves

In Greece, cooks pick fresh vines leaves from their garden, then stuff them with various ingredients, including spicy minced meats. You will need to buy vine leaves from a large supermarket, or from a **delicatessen**. In this version of the dish, the vine leaves are stuffed with rice, herbs, pine nuts and currants. It is a tasty **vegetarian** dish.

What you need

225g packet preserved
   vine leaves

1 onion

2 cloves garlic

2 tbsp olive oil

150g uncooked long
   grain rice

40g pine nuts

40g currants

2 tsp fennel seeds

2 tbsp fresh
   chopped mint

4 tbsp fresh
   chopped parsley

What you do

1 Put the vine leaves in cold water to soak. **Peel** and finely **chop** the onion and garlic.

2 Heat the oil in small saucepan and **fry** the onion and garlic gently for 3 minutes.

3 Tip the onions and garlic into a bowl. Stir in the rice, pine nuts, currants, fennel seeds, mint and parsley.

4 Lay a vine leaf on a board, with the veined side up. Cut off the stalk if it sticks out. Put a heaped teaspoon of the mixture at the stalk end of the leaf.

5 Fold the stalk end of the vine leaf over the filling, fold the sides in and roll up the leaf as tightly as you can.

6 Place the rolled leaf loose end down in a large saucepan or deep-sided frying pan.

7 Repeat steps 4 to 6 until the the pan is covered with tightly packed leaves.

8 Cover the vine leaves with cold water. Put a small stack of plates on top to press down on them. **Cover** the pan and **simmer** for 30 minutes. (Add extra water if the vine leaves start sticking to the pan.)

9 Carefully lift the stuffed vine leaves onto a plate. Serve hot or cold with a little yoghurt.

Spiced rice and lentils

In Greece, rice and lentils are often cooked together with spices. Serve this dish on its own or with **grilled** meat.

What you need

100g brown lentils
2 onions
2 tbsp oil
1 tsp ground cinnamon
½ tsp caraway seeds
75g long grain rice
400g can chopped
　　plum tomatoes
2 tbsp fresh
　　chopped parsley

*To **garnish**:*
a sprig of parsley

What you do

1 Put the lentils into a sieve and hold them under cold, running water. Put them into a large pan and cover with water. (Don't add salt; this makes lentils tough.)

2 Bring the water to the **boil**. Boil the lentils for 10 minutes, then **cover** and **simmer** for 20 minutes. Add some more hot water if the lentils start sticking to the pan.

(!) **3** **Drain** the lentils and put them to one side.

4 **Peel** both onions. **Slice** one and finely **chop** the other.

(!) **5** Heat 1 tbsp of the oil in a large saucepan. **Fry** the chopped onion gently for 5 minutes.

6 Add the cinnamon, caraway seeds and drained lentils to the pan. Stir in the rice, tomatoes and 175ml hot water. Bring to the boil, cover and simmer for 20 minutes.

(!) **7** Heat the remaining oil in a frying pan. Fry the sliced onion until it is crispy.

8 Stir the chopped parsley into the rice and lentil mixture. Put onto a serving dish and garnish with the onion and a sprig of parsley.

Chicken with lemons and olives

Many Greeks have a lemon tree growing in their garden. Greek cooks use lemons in many dishes, both sweet and **savoury**. Lemon leaves are even used to line the base of casserole dishes or pans, to stop food at the bottom from getting too hot.

What you need

4 chicken legs or
  breast portions
½ tsp ground cinnamon
2 onions
3 tbsp olive oil
1 chicken stock cube
1 lemon
few sprigs of fresh thyme
75g pitted black olives
a little salt and pepper

To *garnish:*
sprigs of fresh thyme

What you do

1 **Preheat** the oven to 190°C/375°F/gas mark 5. Cut off any fat or loose skin from the chicken portions.

2 Sprinkle cinnamon, salt and pepper over the skin.

3 **Peel** and **slice** the onions.

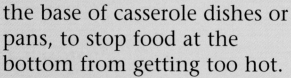

(!) 4 Heat the oil in a frying pan over a medium heat. Add the chicken and onion. **Fry** until the chicken is lightly browned all over.

5 Put the chicken and onions into an ovenproof dish. Crumble the stock cube into 300ml hot water. Carefully pour the stock over the chicken.

6 Cut the lemon into wedges and add them and the thyme to the chicken. Cover the dish and **bake** for 30 minutes.

(!) **7** Carefully lift the dish out of the oven. Stir in the olives, cover and cook for a further 30 minutes.

8 Garnish with the sprigs of thyme. Serve hot.

USING LEMONS

Greek cooks use lemons to add tangy flavour from their skins. Lemon juice makes meat more tender.

Almond cake

The pink blossom of almond trees is a familiar sight all over Greece. Almond cake is often cut into small squares and served with strong, Greek coffee in cafés.

What you need

2 eggs
100ml olive oil
100ml Greek yoghurt
3 tbsp clear honey
100g caster sugar
2 tsp baking powder
100g plain flour
100g ground almonds
25g blanched almonds

What you need

1 **Preheat** oven to 190°C/375°F/gas mark 5. Line the base and sides of a 20cm deep cake tin with non-stick baking paper.

2 To separate the egg yolks from the whites, crack open an egg over a bowl. Keeping the yolk in one half of the shell, let the white drip into the bowl. Pass the yolk between the two halves of the shell until all the white has dripped out. Tip the yolk into a separate bowl. Repeat for the second egg.

3 Put the olive oil, yoghurt and honey into a bowl. Add the two egg yolks and **beat** the mixture until it is smooth.

4 Use an electric whisk to **whisk** the egg whites until they are stiff.

5 **Sift** the caster sugar, baking powder, flour and ground almonds together. Sprinkle them over the olive oil mixture.

6 Using a large metal spoon, gently cut through the mixture to **fold** in the dry ingredients.

7 Add the egg whites and fold them into the mixture with the metal spoon.

8 Spoon the mixture into the cake tin. Smooth the top with the back of a spoon.

9 Holding each blanched almond, carefully **slice** them. Scatter them over the cake.

10 **Bake** on the middle shelf of the oven for 35 to 45 minutes, until the cake springs back when lightly pressed.

11 Let the almond cake **cool** in the tin for 10 minutes. Turn it out onto a wire cooling rack. Serve cut into slices.

Greek yoghurt with honey and fruit

Honey is an important ingredient in Greek cookery. In Greece, fresh fruit such as figs, dates and melon are often served with honey and yoghurt as a simple dessert. The Ancient Greeks believed honey had healing powers. They smoothed it onto cuts and burns. Here, it is used just for its smooth, sweet taste.

What you need

150g Greek yoghurt
3 tbsp clear runny honey
2 figs or 8 dates
100g water melon (about 2 **slices**)

What you do

1 Stir the yoghurt and honey together gently until you can see streaks of honey in all the yoghurt. This is a 'marbled' effect.

2 Wipe the figs and cut them into quarters. If you are using dates, cut them in half, remove the stones and throw them away.

3 Lay the melon flat on a board. Cut the hard green skin off.

4 Arrange the fruit onto two plates. Put a large spoonful of the yoghurt and honey onto each plate. Serve **chilled**.

GREEK HONEY

Bees collect pollen from flowers and take it back to their hives to make honey. The flavour of the honey depends on which flowers the bees visited. Greek honey is dark and runny, with a very rich flavour. The best type comes from the capital city of Greece, Athens. It is called Hymettus honey.

Baklava

What you need

200g shelled
   pistachio nuts
150g blanched almonds
25g shelled walnuts
1 tsp ground cinnamon
¼ tsp ground cloves
50g butter
270g packet filo pastry
6 tbsp clear honey
100g caster sugar
1 cinnamon stick

Baklava is a spicy pastry with honey. In Greece, people traditionally eat it with a cup of strong, Greek coffee. You only need a small piece of baklava. It is extremely sweet!

What you do

1 **Chop** the nuts in a food processor for a few seconds. Put them into a bowl. Add the cinnamon and cloves.

2 **Preheat** the oven to 180°C/350°F/gas mark 4. Put the butter into a small saucepan and heat it gently until it has melted.

3 Using a pastry brush, brush one sheet of filo pastry with melted butter, then fold it in half. Put the rest of the filo pastry sheets under a clean tea towel.

4 Lay the pastry into a 20cm square baking tray, letting any extra pastry hang over the sides. Repeat with another sheet of pastry.

5 Scatter half of the nuts into the baking tray. Level the mixture with a wooden spoon.

6 Cut the remaining pastry into 20cm squares. Brush 3 squares with butter and lay them on top of the nuts. Scatter the rest of the nuts over the pastry.

7 Fold any excess pastry over the nuts. Put any remaining pastry on top, and brush it with melted butter.

8 Cut the top of the baklava carefully into 4cm squares, but don't let the knife cut all the way through to the baking tray.

9 **Bake** for 25 minutes. Meanwhile, put the honey, sugar, cinnamon stick and 100ml water into a small pan. Heat them gently until the sugar has **dissolved**.

(!) 10 Pour the liquid over the hot baklava. Leave it to cool completely for 1 hour. Cut all the way through into squares to serve.

Lemonade

Lemons grow in many areas of Greece and are used in many recipes. This is a very popular drink, especially during the long, hot Greek summers. Use unwaxed lemons, if you can. Otherwise, scrub the lemon skins very well with warm water to remove any wax.

What you need

2 lemons
60g sugar

What you do

1 Using a vegetable peeler, **peel** the yellow skin off 1 lemon. (Try not to peel too much of the white pith which is attached to the skin, because it will make the lemonade bitter.) Put the peel into a large, heatproof jug.

2 Cut both lemons in half. Using a lemon squeezer, squeeze the juice from the lemons.

3 Put the lemon juice and sugar into the heatproof jug with the peel.

4 Measure 600ml **boiling** water into a measuring jug and pour over the peel. Stir well, cover with a clean tea towel and leave to **cool**. When it is cold, **chill** the lemonade overnight in the fridge.

5 Put a sieve over a wide-necked jug. Pour the lemonade through the sieve. Taste the juice and add a little extra sugar, if you wish.

6 Pour into two glasses and add some sparkling water, if you like. Serve chilled.

HOT AND COLD

Never put hot foods into a fridge to cool down. The heat from the hot food will warm up the other items in the fridge, making them go off more quickly. Always cool hot foods to room temperature first, and then chill them.

Further information

Here are some places to find out more about Greece and Greek cooking.

Books

A Visit to Greece
Peter Roop, Heinemann Library, 1999.
Greece
Julia Waterlow, Wayland 1991
Real Greek Food
Theodore Kyriakou and Charles Campion, Pavilion, 2000.
A Taste of the Greek Islands
Pamela Westland, Letts of London, 1992.

Websites

www.greekcuisine.com
www.greece.com/directory/recreation/food

Conversion chart

Ingredients for recipes can be measured in two different ways. Metric measurements use grams and millilitres. Imperial measurements use ounces and fluid ounces. This book uses metric measurements. The chart here shows you how to convert measurements from metric to imperial.

SOLIDS		LIQUIDS	
METRIC	**IMPERIAL**	**METRIC**	**IMPERIAL**
10g	¼ oz	30ml	1 fl oz
15g	½ oz	50ml	2 fl oz
25g	1 oz	75ml	2½ fl oz
50g	1¾ oz	100ml	3½ fl oz
75g	2¾ oz	125ml	4 fl oz
100g	3½ oz	150ml	5 fl oz
150g	5 oz	300ml	10 fl oz
250g	9 oz	600ml	20 fl oz
450g	16 oz	1 litre	30½ fl oz

Healthy eating

This diagram shows you which foods you should eat to stay healthy. Most of your food should come from the bottom of the pyramid. Eat some of the foods from the middle every day. Only eat a little of the foods from the top.

Healthy eating, Greek-style

The Greek diet is very healthy, because it includes lots of fresh fruit and vegetables, rice, grains and fish. Meat is eaten less often. Cooks use olive oil for cooking, which is healthier than other fats. Greek yoghurt can contain about 10% fat compared to 2–3% fat in most fruit-flavoured yoghurts. Greek cakes and pastries are very sweet, so they should only be enjoyed from time to time!

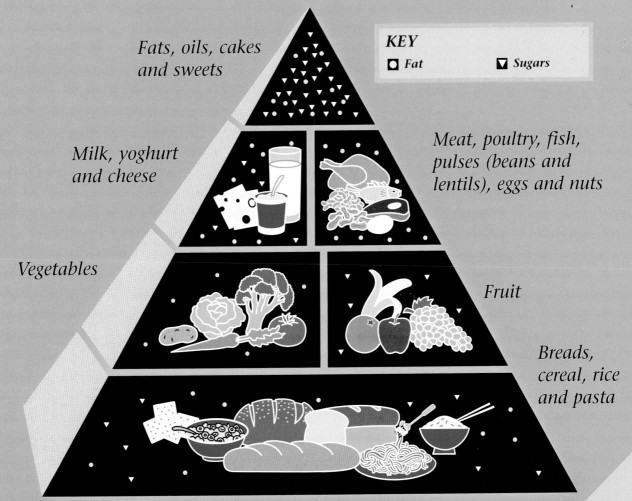

Fats, oils, cakes and sweets

KEY
◻ *Fat* ▽ *Sugars*

Milk, yoghurt and cheese

Meat, poultry, fish, pulses (beans and lentils), eggs and nuts

Vegetables

Fruit

Breads, cereal, rice and pasta

Glossary

bake cook something in the oven

beat mix something together strongly, for example, egg yolks and whites

blend mix ingredients together in an electric blender or food processor

boil cook a liquid on the hob. Boiling liquid bubbles and steams strongly.

chill put a dish into the fridge for several hours before serving

chop cut something into pieces using a knife

cool allow hot food to become cold. You should always allow hot food to cool before putting it in the fridge.

cover put a lid on a pan, or foil over a dish

delicatessen shop or counter that sells special foods and delicassies

dissolve mix something, for example sugar, until it disappears into a liquid

drain remove liquid, usually by pouring something into a colander or sieve

dressing oil and vinegar sauce for salad

fold mix dry ingredients into a wet mixture using cutting movements with a metal spoon. This keeps more air in the mixture.

fry cook something in oil in a pan

garnish decorate food, for example, with fresh herbs or lemon wedges

grill cook something under a grill

marinade soak foods, especially meat or fish, in a liquid to add flavour

mash crush something, for example, potatoes, until soft and pulpy

pasteurized milk that has been heated to a high temperature and then cooled, to kill any germs in it

peel remove the skin of a fruit or vegetable

preheat turn on the oven in advance, so that it is hot when you put food into it

savoury the opposite of sweet. Savoury dishes may contain meat, fish, eggs or cheese.

sift pass dry ingredients through a sieve to remove any lumps

simmer cook liquid on the hob. Simmering liquid bubbles and steams gently.

slice cut something into thin flat pieces

thaw defrost something which has been frozen

toast cook something in a pan without any oil in it

vegetarian food which does not contain meat or fish. People who don't eat meat or fish are called vegetarians.

whisk mix ingredients using a whisk

Index